Everyday Stories

by
Tammy M. Jones
aka
Poetry's Child

Everyday Stories
Copyright © 2011 by Tammy M. Jones
tammyjonespoetry@yahoo.com

Cover design by MsNess
Vanessa Pacheco for iFS Graphics
iflowsoul@gmail.com

Published by Tammy M. Jones for Hip Hope Publishing
tammyjonespoetry@yahoo.com

ISBN-978-0-9834739-0-9

the day is long bringing a midnight's sun
at the end of the day and it's still not done
feeling the burden on my back when mostly
I need to relax
the facts prove I need a break and a broken back
isn't the take I seek

my heart leaks of depression, confession couldn't
calm its beats
music plays to the cadence of my reason
treason by another wouldn't feel punishment
enough for my iniquities

strictly I pursue to pay my dues
since the woes of time won't leave me
loosed to the wolves of suffering
at the end of my days as time ticks
so do the coattails of my clothing fray
I live to see the sun shine another day where I,
as a child, get to play again on the marsh by the sea
where seeing is believing we are all God's children
no matter what the humans say

tmj

A Note To The Reader

If you have bought my book and hold it in your hands reading this now, I thank you for supporting my craft and hope you have intentions to read the tickings of my poetic heart and thoughts that ride the brain waves in my head. There is a method to the madness and it comes out through projects such as this because truly a poet breathes in hopes to just be heard, as my heart desires and those of others like me. I hope you enjoy this work and it leaves you a bit outside your comfort zone after reading because this world we live in isn't always what it seems. I pray this book inspires you to go out, take action, and make a difference on Poverty Street in Anytown, USA.

This book is dedicated to the world and anyone who understands Hip Hope...my kids and all the poets who inspire others to do something out of necessity to make it better...

The Belly Of The Beast

There's something going on in the storm way out of the norm
that messes up the reception of my dreams
causing me to scream out of tune like a loon or a wolf howling at
the moon
but I know despite what happens, it's going to break real soon

It's the money, the pain, and the hurt and the dance with life that
started out with simple words from a flirtatious
deception one never ever thought to mention

The recession has made a procession from the west to the east,
where it's a showdown in the belly of the beast and the screaming
never ceases as volume increases the creases in foreheads
Lines leading nomads to nomadic lands founded in the sands
where survival is minimal and a fool will get his fill of pride
guiding him blind on a grind of frustration
Fatality seems to be the penalty to pay for a way out of the
maze
trying to find a route hasn't phased a face in amazing ways
or hours at a time, if but only for a few seconds of a dream,
as you can once again hear the cries like someone just died,
that sound never lies how lives are lost and the cost for a loss
dictates as boss

The bottom of the barrel when you hit rock bottom has a
growl of an empty stomach and the thoughts in your head
that run like a movie, are the reminders of why living life with
blinders is dangerous
and in the end if we are still standing we hope to meet a
thing called justice
When it's served we hope to be able to hear that
uttered word...

G U I L T Y...

Guilty is Wall Street and every irresponsible financial institution
that
played out the scam in this major illusion, who now owe
the tax payers restitution, for allowing America to get caught
with her skirt in the air hoeing for cheap deals under the Bush
umbrella giving major ass up to the corporations who corp-a-

raped her
Scraped her knees on the floor of a concrete jungle as she
struggled to understand the downfall of the American Dream and
how she fell apart all at the seams
but the devious kings of corporate America
sold houses and cars to people with no money down and we
wonder how we ran her into the ground
It's the greatest Ponzi scheme of all ripping up the means of
Americans, who felt free to dream

Sighs muffle muttered cries knowing for every car and house
divided were the reasons we bragged united
Wheew, the American Dream turned into sneaky schemes, where
man made money out the side of the family
As expected, he got a slap on the hand for the deception,
as if the exception granted him a victory
Well now we stand knee high in floods with waves that get
rough in the such and such's that define the BS of life
that breaks decrees by men with degrees as we continue
to drown at sea without a life preserver

The Terrorism Files

Safety kits have changed to a bulletproof vest instead of band-
aids in a chest
and our backyards now take on the external wall of our home
Due to terrorism, there's not far we can roam, outdoors are not
allowed
The ravens flying overhead, as a dark cloud, are waiting to attack
without rest
and we live our lives attempting to pass tests
Anyone, as close as even a neighbor, wearing a scarf to hide his
face can be a terrorist and slip into our homeland without trace
Terrorism has sucked the freedom right out of the bell, as it rings
stale
The eagle flies high and for freedom our voices, as Americans,
sing fear through our land this terrorist threat now brings

We, one as a people, down on our knees to pray without delay
asking our Father in the heavens for a brighter day

Our president keeps us overseas fighting a war we still haven't
won, as troops are equipped with a knapsack and a gun

RUN! as bombs drop! RUN! as bombs drop!
we can't stop the madness
sadness of death, sadness of scenes seen by eyes raw, the
scalding of reality, the realness they saw

Mauled is flesh by bombs and guns, troops on the run for lives
scribed to face a penance without sin screaming souls within a
soldier's chest
No rest for the weary, dreary be the skies disguised by a new
day's sunrise
Lies told, as false prophets behold their own ideas taken from the
book of Revelations for profits
The Bible scribed becomes a game of scrabble, where men take
their own interpretations to define life and call strife a plague
from the book to stir a false consciousness that consists of no
more than lies
Flies stalk us because wounds are formed by the very everyday
way we live life
Words stab like knives and change this first amendment that
claims freedom of speech but like leeches, we suck blood to

lessen one's self worth to get ahead
led by tongues of fire, more on fire to burn a being, considered to
be an obstacle
Topical cream won't smooth wrongs right so with one another we
continue to fight to make the ball of chaos stronger and faster in
its flight to kill off the world

The terrorists do not live in Afghanistan, Iraq, or a place where
one is stationed to set off bombs
Someone told each of us we be da bomb because verbally we are
bombing isht with our own words, actions and thoughts taking
out humanity day by day, still our will to be the best at least
When the freedom bell still rings stale, 41 shots ring out in a hail
and we are walking around feeling sorry so frail, as if victims we
be to society,
just remember how we pick and choose our fights and it started
out as a non-vote coming from the mouth of one who gloats how
they won't cast a word of yeah or nay on election day

the devil's game (inspired by Va Tech)

eyes glazed with death
scent of rot on his breath
the devil in disguise pulling
off another body snatching
heads left with hands scratching
wondering what just happened
after the guns stop clapping
smacking high fives with Lucifer
silence
the stench in the trench
now a battlefield was once a
learning zone
bad to the bone skin deep,
evil creeps in the form of GI Joe
free styling with magazine clips and
hollow point tips
rage bubbling flips
mad man on the rise as bodies lay
lifeless
he went nuts for the hell of this

guilty thoughts permeate the air he
absorbs
3rd eye awakens, he's now shaken to the scene
before him
slim chance for negotiation, he'll do a tour on
death row, indictable is this crime
for a second he lost his mind taking on actions of
mimes he so thought
caught and ashamed, heated is the blame, the
corruption of an untamed beast
at the very least with no options he picks up a hand gun
and puts it to his head, pulls the trigger, he falls dead
as Lucifer smacks him a high five with a big hug as another
pawn falls

Krackers Krumble

minority reports
escort a prysmatic team
dream
schemed to be the underdog
krackers krumble
as they attempt to stumble
diversity at the knee
the fee paid as knee deep laid
out
krackers have the upper hand
in this bout says they
but the underdog can't sway to the canvas
for an eight count
doubt is the clout rocked by a rainbow
of positivity dropping divinity on a **new**
word order

slaughtered is the lamb by G-men who
run the land and hide behind white militia
who are paid to take their stand
with gun in hand and sheets over head looking
like Casper the ghost to haunt sacred sands
where blood trails have long dried and the salt
from eyes that cried become the seeds sown
to reap a plenty in abundance of strength
where brinks of break broke on the tongue
of blame that burns to pass shame and
take over America without true facts

just simply opinion to back the words of
a kracker krumbled
tip toeing on cracks
attacks by 'out of work' minds that won't twerk
more brain dead because their people inbreed
the steed that replicates a public school system
that tax dollars don't free
krackers krumble and Americans pay double
shackled at the ankle swollen cankles with rings

around bones defining years of oppression of the
new school creed
deeds done dirty of destructive seeds concede
openly of thievery that pushed Indians out of
chivalry

krackers krumble, as weak men lose minds led
blindly on the grind fueled by passion and the
desires of a white house resident's visions to
defeat and cheat the land owners as he stands
full of conceit
lily white stained lies, as though the people didn't
see how true selfishness greeds for now but in
the end that kracker will krumble as he dies
suffocating in a pool of blood dipped in HIV

I Wanna Read A Poem (inspired by Def Poet, Steve Colman)

I wanna read a poem that explains top conspiracies as to why
piracy is a crime yet someone lied avoiding time

i.e. katrina, 9/11, the threats of assassination on Barack Obama
before the DNC

I wanna read a poem that talks of green acred lands that doesn't
have stuff under the carpet swept as the dirt
of rumors leaving ulcerated bumps from a slump
that caught publicity

i.e. the lack of interest from the Board of Ed in city schools
and the money being spent on weekend trysts instead of books

I wanna read a poem that shows people on same planes instead
of some stained by the strain of racist ways as lain out by this
country's 'humanly' ways

i.e. police brutality, lack of healthcare, proper education
for everyone regardless of where you live

I wanna read a poem that attempts to understand instead of
expand on the ignorance of 'trying to help others' when we need
to help a sister or brother

i.e. homeless people, rebound from natural disaster, and
educating today's children to be our future

I wanna read a poem where a child with a special talent is
given a gallant effort to mold something into gold instead
of being pimped and sold

i.e. the music industry

I wanna read a poem that shows acceptance of different life
styles made by choice and a man/woman to walk a mile in

another person's shoes before judgment is passed, assault is
committed and a name is trashed for Nosy's pleasure

I wanna read a poem that allows children to have career picks as
choices instead of voices filling heads that say fast
money is what they need instead

I wanna read a poem where candy-swirled dreams fill minds as
they sleep to wake to a grind of reality and the birth of desires,
where fire is the flame of motivation to one day see the elevation
of prosperity

I wanna read a poem!!!!!

Chaos Makes Us

chaos
makes us
exactly what we are today
the fray of material, the wear of disarray
the fade in a hue, the dying of a truth
the Book of Revelations screams the proof
People up in arms when they should pray to not be harmed
The Muslims, Christians, and Jews and the stories in the news
The fighting in the middle east when all should hope for peace
The threat of terrorism spreads like a disease out of control,
which has much to do with the politicians we pick at the polls
When we dance with the devil, our soul sure is sold

chaos
makes us
exactly what we are today
the fray of material, the wear of disarray
1st amendment rights to speak our own minds on a grind,
as they tap our phones like we are 3rd eye blind
There was never a new amendment that was taught in school
that said the government could use our rights as a tool
to fool us into believing they secure our best interest,
when they look at us as animals more than less

I write to recite messages dropping bombs to make you think
but instead of encouragement the government would leave me
extinct and kill off our freedom of speech because truly a poet
steps on toes to preach and teach the troubles of this world

chaos
makes us
exactly what we are today
the fray of material, the wear of
disarray
Homeland security went out a back door
Took a tour of duty and never returned from that war
The score of hits America has withstood makes living
in the hood sound good
Despite the oxymoron we know that to be,
we live in America, the home of the free
where many have degrees but we don't have jobs

because the government runs isht like the mob
Allowing companies to send our positions overseas,
as if we nodded our heads all to agree
Look at the backbone of the car industry,
we now have to sell the companies overseas
just to save the grieving economy

chaos
makes us
exactly what we are today
the fray of material, the wear of disarray
The ozone is dying and our weather isn't right,
as we tear down the forest to build new homes and
the animals have no place to roam
More people have cell phones and eventually cancer
of the brain will leave millions deaf without tone
Back in the day, they said technology was the key
but the more advanced we become, the environment bleeds
crying of pain and suffering
To our own children, what will this bring?
The planet is dying as they claim earth could exist another 80
years, as we continue to kill off resources without a care

chaos
makes us
exactly what we are today

no better than we were a time before

It Was All A Dream

It was all a dream and reality seeped into the seams
of the clouded frames, as goodness was sought in
the arena of thought

The children still don't have enough food to eat
Skeet, skeet, they are victims of repetitive crimes
light in the alleys and stairwells never shines
and darkness leads the blind to feel, where only
coldness dwells
Prostitution and drugs are retail and each face

is real with a name attached lacking definitions
of goals and dreams caught up in the hoopla of
the negativity

Clinically people walk around insane and brain
dead
Bodies so malnourished, never fed of spirituality,
hopes and goals
In the war zone, hearts will roam seeking the somethings
they don't realize they desire
Confusion tags a toe to a brain uninspired to be led by
a positive model
More likely they will get drunk off the bottle
of a liquored world
where blurs are made up of swirls of not comprehended
colors and patterns
and lost souls become gathered in one place where
rock bottom is the only direction the elevator will go

It was all a dream and reality seeped into the seams of the
clouded frames, as goodness was sought in the arena of thought

Caught up on a common plateau, the mistake--that we are
all on the same page
More like either free or caged and caged means you're free as far
as the limitations of a box and beyond those lines

Confined is the darkness where the line is drawn and
nothingness fills a being's void and a soul becomes destroyed
never understanding the reality of the outside world past
that which left us tied to a steel ball
Once a death warms over, the same ball will be tossed into a lake,
which may be fire or that image could be fake
that all bad souls burn at the stake
For heaven's sake, there is a God and for Him we breathe
regardless of the leashes that hold us all back, we all live

life under an attack
but without a dream to dream, life is lifeless and to the
devil we give the glory
and when the last breath bleeds so does his story that
started out as a dream
It busted at the seams, as clouded frames of goodness
in the arena of thought
A victory is sought seeking the Father to be the reality
where we are caught knowing
we are His children and protected from that evil one

Mr. President, Holler If You Hear Me

The goals u conceived to be attainable seem unstable in a time,
where an economy rests on 3 legs unable to believe your dream
Though u have a confidence that seems different and your
intentions are good as they should be
I don't see where you're going because of past history
You keep telling us it will take time and we have to stay in line
with the plan
and take a stand 2 weather storms because seeing the worst
before it gets better is the norm the images my mind
continues to form
I think u can see the veins of fear as they appear on the face
of 'Hell No' as it leers like a shadow rougher than a
jet of turbulence
At times forgive me but I'd rather sit on a fence of freelance
than take a stance for socialism with my journalistic views
Just know despite it all I'm still behind you 100%
because others before you never did the job they
were suppose to perform

Mr. President, holler if u hear me

Healthcare is a wear and tear on derogatory times to stay alive
The government ferments in a batch of pharmaceuticals where
white-collar thugs create conspiracies of a pandemic plateau
The masses are watching through the eyes of a lighthouse sifting
through the outlines of an apparitional shroud
knowing back alleys pave the way of solution for suffering
Vaccinations are activating the rumors that blow to the
level of doubt
where the clout of the medical field shouts devious deeds
that clot the bleeding with the results it brings
Leading us in faith to have trust that they didn't inject us
with the death injection to look famous with the remedy
for that same infection
Mr. President, do u feel me? because buying healthcare
packages at my job leaves me feeling robbed
Like what did I just buy and will it keep me alive
in the midst of the underhandedness of an underworld

Mr. President, holler if u hear me
Terrorism alerts are at an all time high and living your
life with eyes open bloodied is a 24/7 of anyone breathing sighs
Foreign policy cries from the pit where pangs of war are scored
on the grounds in the belly of the beast where doors are locked
and knobs that turn are a tour of duty
As a country pulling together and looking left at the government
and right at the strangers who imitate the dangerous don't
soothe me
I thank God Hilary won over Sarah for a position in a president's
cabinet
because that fool from Iceland wasn't clear and we weren't
having it
Regardless we live life walking on landmines praying we don't
become
the prey per say
Safety is conveyed as a job description of homeland security
but there's a weakest link that squeeks as a bad cog in the wheel,
when paid, reveals all the G-men claim they do for me
Where do we go when tax dollars get tied up in the hands
of heads paid who don't give a damn if we die?

Mr. President, holler if u hear me

Choose Life

it's the way it is
people are homeless
hungry and dying
some lead a life of crime
growing up in the big house

while others...

try to make it, raise a family as
they seek relief

color is nothing but preference for a racist
issues overwhelm all people
we all cry, laugh, and die
as humans, let's choose life

helping a sister, brother, each other
to make it
we can't fake seeing things
working together we can break molds
let the bad men fold and raise one another's
hand in victory

this thought is surreal
helping a hungry man get a meal
blinders conceal true issues in
a community
we need to breathe air for unity
I know you feel this because I'm not
talking junk
feel my beat, tap your foot, sing
words to my song
but whatever, let's all belong to
the one cause
down for human beings
choose life and extend a hand to the

person standing next to you
because the next in need could be you

Prophetic Nightmares

I have prophetic nightmares that warn me to stay clear
of my fears
Tears are the cleansing of wounds where a healing soothes
a pained heart
A balm like psalms on Sunday, where hymns are sang sweet
preacher like stanky gospel choir style

Riled are the troops then coup d'etat
people fret running the streets wondering what comes next
Selective become choices from voices that crack with panic
due to manic disturbia
The walls of ghetto Poland echo in every corner on Hitler's list
taking the innocence of Anne Frank and putting it back on our
streets
where children are 'X' marked by violence through gang wars,
recession, and families where a parent has lost a job suffering
with necessity
As the people within the walls of Poland cried with bellies so
swollen, that led to stolen thoughts of being fed on deception
the same, as our government, becomes bent on burying a white
collar crime in an unmarked tomb

Conception of better ways to avoid mortality is where I tend to
crave doom in my dreams so when I wake, reality sets in,
etched in stone,
where I laid in a grave next to bones to the tune of 'Dead Man
Walking' in a departure zone
Moans, jeers and high pitched cries are the proof that I'm still
alive as I roll on my side to take in the ruins I view

I rise to my feet standing toe to toe with Lestat glaring at me
through cold icy gray eyes, as if I was his Queen of the Damned
Ran, I did, as I shot like a bullet across the dark eery cemetery,

where plots made up scams to pull me in, I suspected the sin of it
all
I had no idea what I did to sense the grasp of abduction for the
structure of my mind was a makeshift caper of what the end
would reveal
so fear would steal my soul as the grim reaper came peering
down upon me, he whispered, "what is your soul worth?"

It is worth the birth of pains my mother endured to bring me
here and valued highly to fight you to the death, as I may,
take my last breath and look you in the eyes so you can despise
the goodness of my soul

His face was nil beneath the black hood, where darkness
replicated emptiness and literally filled the Reaper's skull
invisible
yet, the intensity of his immoral ways respired the stench
of decaying brains
leaving the fill of insanity stained on my heart as I strained
to see the smile on his face and the strength of his laugh,
was laced with greed

Mentally I vision the very scenes of the cemetery, the soldiers
marching, the eyes of Lestat, the walls of Poland and Anne
Frank's diary, the children of America who have no idea what it
means to have a dream
and the people who suffered victim at the hands of a Ponzie
scheme and how it's the government choking us that makes eye
sockets bleed
blinding us to not be able to follow our dreams to one day be
successful and JUST BE FREE!!

Death In A Bottle (inspired by Poetic Devotion)

I feel like dying, I feel LIKE dying, I feel LIKE DYING
having fell to the bottom of a bottle looking up
through the spout screaming shouts no one can hear
nor would they come near if they knew a fool was
drowning in the brew

An alcoholic river yet it was a mental endeavor that
brought me this fight now fought and since that I'm
in too deep, I'm restless and can't sleep
My pen be fly when it cries but I'd rather be like
Helen Keller and be unfeeling like the coldest cellar
where I may find the next bottle, where I swallow
a glass whole swole, my belly is coated numb

I feel like dying, I feel LIKE dying, I feel LIKE DYING
cause people around me are dying as they
are lying in the puddle of poverty victims of
a system that they all supported with tax
dollars, as they were grabbed by the collar
and treated like they committed a crime
As time passed they stay locked up for
nothing more than a 'boys' in blue escapade'
and as I lay in my bed at night I can't sleep
because isht isn't right
people are dying, yes, they ARE dying, the
people are dying for lack of food, for being
jobless will not fill a belly full
the fat lady is singing and the bell is
taking its toll ringing out of control

I feel like dying, I feel LIKE dying, yes, I feel LIKE DYING,
as Uncle Sam stays co-signing the ways of the world
and if drinking another bottle didn't cost me tax
and fill Sam's pocket with change
I'd allow my deranged mind to release its fear

drowning in the drool of a fool's drink as I sink
to new lower heights out of sight, where tears
get released and a new piece flows from my pen
and I can breathe again despite the people are
dying and I readjust to a new level of acceptable
acceptance, where dreams die because the people
remain bent

In The Name Of Karma

despite the pouring rain I try to refrain from doing
dark alley things but the thunder and dark cloud
bring all the negative in bad dreams that haunt my
head
they lead me by the hand, as people whisper
and bad rumors about me are being said
God lets us go through events to wake us up and
hear His voice because humanly by choice he is
last on our lists
Getting a grip on the change in events got me wanting
to grab my pen and vent but it was from He who I
received my gift and I'm suppose to use it to uplift
another person going through something
The street loves to see a person going through the
bad, as if laughing, at another's bad luck was a
sport
As if it couldn't happen to you and your home
and security was a fort locked down and safe
Yeah right! You may be the next in line because
the last days are here and we have to face our
fears and chaos knows no color
We all got a part in the struggle and going through
some trouble
Lend a hand and pick up a person so they don't have
to suffer doubled over with tears being the only
way they communicate
Fate has a way of playing against the grain, as the train
comes full speed to stop on the edge of bleeding knees
and the only way to not feel pain is to freeze your heart
and put a bricked wall around it as it beats
Defeat is a bitch and nothing for pockets filled but it
seems if you have a rich soul and love passionately
it finds its way in the door to your home
As it scratches at the surface and pecks away like
the enemy at your goodness and it watches you

die slowly in the name of Karma

Visions That Plague

rainbow schemes of dreams,
nightmares wake me
at the stake awake, I'm stoked
as if high on coke
and church folk try and ring my
bell
disguised the devil in hell
I'm in a 9 foot cell sold on thoughts
bought from not knowing myself
more stalked on lonely
stone-ly becomes my face, a reality's
disgrace
the face a blind man sees in his head
instead I'm dread of heartbreak and pain
the stain of blasphemy's strains
I can't take these mental and physical
chains no more
I was born to a life where at times, I'd
rather be dead
but instead I live and have no courage to
take my life, as I ponder ways to shed
the skin of strife
life being hard got me at times dreaming
of the afterlife
as I pray the streets are made of gold and
boldness is not a characteristic you need
just the fact you were a seed planted and
you bloomed allowing God to use you in
His grand scheme of things brings me hope

He lifts me up to look into His eyes and say,
"child, do you not hear my very words of
verse where I've conversed leaving a bible
in the hands of this universe?
I gave you what you needed and many times

repeated to remind you of your talents and
to use them gallantly but you take off your
blinders and get bent on finding things that
don't exist among the masses, where life
moves too fast
Don't get gassed up on craziness just feel the
bliss of my tenderness as I treat you with the
kid gloves and show you my love"
and while I'm here I scope my angle of this
thing called hip hope, where God handed me
this pen and pad and I scribe things of bad
and good and wait on the inspiration of He,
who saved me, to drop a lesson learned on
the masses and let them know what I go
through is similar to what they also go
through and somehow we will make it
through together

The people suffering without clothes or food
and the man or woman without a job, who
were robbed 9 out of 10 times, by G-Men ways
wondering in this fabricated line where the
government doesn't give a damn as tax payers
keep this land
this will be considered really bad when
they can't keep feeding themselves on
bullshit once we are all unemployed
and on the unemployment line joined
hands willing to do more
it will be a white sheet faces verses
a rainbow coalition of all out havoc
and chaos because the people can't
take no more, the people can't take
no more, NO we can't take it!

as the feet will hit the floor running
in the last days where robbing, looting

and suffering will be acceptable as a
way of life
and the poets will sit back watching
the warnings in their dreams prevail

America, Home Of The Free

The word ridden means 'to be overburdened with' but I'm so
damn sure they meant it differently when cops unloaded
50 bullets into Sean Bell's car the day he died
They were acquitted April 25, 2008,
three of NYC's finest walk free and the masses shook
their heads disbelievingly
Now almost 2 years and change later the same 3 walk
free in a civil case
$7 million is all it cost to get them off
Sean Bell is still in the ground silenced, not one sound
What price was paid for a body needing to be laid to rest?
and what's worse, it was to be the happiest day of his life
Instead his wife had to hear the strife, as cops said he
sucked his last breath and we killed him
Well, I'm sure they attempted to be politically correct
but what the heck, they should have just said it the way
it really happened and it would have been understood
clearly what they meant to say
It had to be quite difficult for the boys in blue to
decide what to do
Sweep it under the carpet but what a bump that made
They created a raid to find a gun that didn't exist and
Sean and his boys were blacklisted stereotyped to be
hype assed gangsta types

I didn't know Sean Bell personally nor did I know if
he was a stand up guy
but I know one thing, no one had to die
Especially in a hail of 50 bullets as the cops sit happy
telling lies and cover for each other constantly
The boys in blue are all they will be
they should be professional enough to be men
in uniform and obey
the norm following all the rules as we do
As they get honored when shot on duty, they should

be rammed up the behind with a night stick when they
do wrong because on these streets even my white ass
doesn't want to roam
Today in 2010, it seems money is the only right color to be,
as long as you're money that brings honey to the hive
In the den of five oh, you can flow on through so freely

Living in these days nothing phases me anymore
especially crime regarding the police of EVERYTOWN, USA
People need to stick together regardless of the way things
are done
The multi faceted rainbow has to stick together instead
of claiming culture barriers that ties the stench of flies
isht isn't easy but standing as one against the wrongdoers
is a start
Katrina still doesn't sit well with me while Mr. Bush flew
overhead in Air Force 1 with a puppy on his lap licking
his crotch
as he had the gall to say he flew over and witnessed
the damage
He blamed Ray Nagin when he didn't call for help but
did anyone actually have to ask for any?
What kind of administration runs this country
where we swear in God we trust, as their response is
a bust on trust when it comes to wheeling and dealing
to care for a natural disaster in our own country
I can get down with helping other countries but
tax payers come first despite we know that will
never happen
Mouths get to flapping on what a great place America is
while red necks and the boys in blue continue to walk
free with a gun in their hand to get bullet happy and
take out the next one
America the free and home of the brave
how I crave to proudly die with her flag
waving high over me

Real Facts On Real Times

I have a 9 to 5 that pays a salary with benefits to boot
but I feel a bit robbed once I count up the leftover loot
After paying taxes and bills and payroll deductions for insurance,
both car and medical and retirement got me with the thoughts
of a radical,
wondering when the poetic revolution will make its debut
Metal screws in my back every payday got me wishing death just
to fade away
Speechless and seeking new ways to keep money in the bank got
me from filling up my tank
It's more like a food for thought and my thoughts won't pay real
bills
No one buys poetry books or a CD with cool hooks but you might
find your isht being sold on a corner in the hood,
where whispered words blow in the breeze for 3 bucks a CD
A M A Z E D is my mind so hard I grind to perfect my craft as a
poet with a pen with a voice to give a voice to the voiceless with
verbs to act
 I'm stacked in knowledge of pronouns, regular nouns and
adjectives
describing scenes where I get agitated on isht like inflation that
deflates my groove because the real crooks sweep realness under
a carpet to hide real truths
I'm not good with substitutes because I'm quite brand loyal as I
took organizational behavior in school to realize I am selective
when choosing words for a message to the masses
I stay gassed up on Websters to weather real storms
I've been described as a rebel because I refuse to choke on the
bullshit of fake tunes

Well back to my dilemma, I have no stamina to continue living in
a country founded on ill promises with crosses to bear with no
paybacks
Attacked is my money jacked up every pay period like
menstruation

I bleed and my seeds go lacking what I can't afford
More, More, More! is what I hear in the air but it isn't fair being
one of the middleclass most likely lower class after the weekly
funeral mass held at the cathedral that prays on hard times and
where is God while we fight to stay alive?
Like I stand repeating myself, poverty knows no color, we're all
poor mother flowers that fight each day to strive

Why does one rich person win the lottery when $43 million is the
pot? Why does Wall Street continue to give top execs big
bonuses after the problems we are still pulling through?
Then they act shocked when Obama catches them and they have
to give it back
Why is it America still didn't fix those levees in Nawlins and why
are people still suffering down in the Bayou?
Why is being a doctor today overrated but insurance companies
are not punished for raising rates?
Why do we get less for more and I buy catheters with cash at the
medical supply store?

anyone got the answers? because I can't fathom the reason we're
fienin for basics and if we are unsuccessful...statistics rise in
deaths and crime is down because people won't give anyone the
pleasure so they JUST DIE NOW!

Dirty David

He may be blind but he knows just what he does
Creeping in the darkness through every space
shaking down tax payers like he was the mob
maybe John Gotti or a Genovese or Gambino
He's no bambino to crime making others pay,
while he should do the time

David Paterson hasn't given one taste bud
reason to believe in him
From the beginning, he went out on a whim
and spoke honestly of indiscretions
The taste was stale
Shoot, didn't we deal with that in President
Clinton but honestly when Clinton was in
the White House, democrats had money
in their pockets and the economy was good
who he had under the desk doing him didn't
take an ounce of money out of me so why
should people care if you cheated on your
wife?
and NOW, you got Davidgate working with
his aide, David Johnson trying to cover Mr.
Johnson's dirty tracks or should I say palm
prints on the face left as traces of domestic
abuse
The governor so powerful had to let loose
and get involved
instead of indict a man for what he himself
has so gallantly spoken against
He supports him and tries to pull a Jason Williams
and cover up the scene
He even sends 2 staff members of his team
to speak to this woman so she won't scream
issues too loud because holy cow, Governor
Paterson can't take any more negative attention
SMH, isn't this some isht, the woman dropped
the charges
I wonder what it took
Did the governor have a gun placed to her head?
Was she hung outside a window by an ankle

with a view of the ground below?
I can't believe a nice little get together with
tea soothed it all better
I know a fair weather friend reared an ugly head
and wished this lady dead if she didn't keep her
mouth shut.
Oops I forgot, she didn't even show up for court
and the case got thrown out
In my eyes, as I mentioned before, David Paterson
is a white collar criminal threatening victims as if
he was a mob boss lying about I did nothing wrong
nor will I resign and the world all sees what he tries
to pull off as he truly claims to be blind

Generation X

crack and the school system
plague my town
and have me running south
for better weather
sunnier, sunny days
more relaxed ways
so I may drop my attitude of an
urban heart

a new start
new address, clean air, better schools
where drugs are controlled more
a score isn't the latest action of
every second I breathe air

scared will be shaken from my heart and
soul knowing I raise children
making it to 18 drug free and alive
are a main goal
anything else is a gift in blessings
from God
swampy sod only pollutes the brain
leaving the heart of a souljah drained
trusting is a must right now
I don't sleep and weep from tiredness
keeping my eyes open and on my children
as they grow free in their minds behind
the physical bars I place to keep them
safe from harm
my soul is alarmed needing a break
before I suffer heart attack

gun shots blow my mind
with pimps and pushers on the grind
that make an honest person lose it all
to be deaf, dumb and blind
pretending to know nothing more
having lost that game in score as the
world continues to turn as tears burn
for the death of a young generation,
whoever happens to be left

Who Has The Right? (inspired by Tribal Raine)

Despite a person has died
who has the right to decide
another's death
This is a lethal chain reaction
and proof of the devil at work

one man dies
his family cries
his killer is jailed
game not over
another murder unveiled
for public viewing

What makes it right for a man
to say if another man should die
To me, this is an evil chain that
leaves blood stains on all involved

Whether you did the initial killing,
was part of the jury and judge who decided
death would bring justice,
was the man to pull the lever or
inject a lethal injection,
we all are part of an infection
spreading virus like fire, no care

I don't believe God is looking down
upon us with love in His eyes
believing what we do is right

When the executioner dies
he may be in for surprise,
God doesn't compromise
the executioner's song will play,
as the hood hangs over his head
in shame

The juror who voted for death
will be questioned about the motive
to rule in favor of killing
choking on his/her own last bit of breath

Who are we mere human beings
to decide such factors
as breathing breath of a condemned man
who got life?

Wake Up!

arms folded on strike
America, it's a wakeup call
my pen lays on its side
and refuses to scribe
we're on strike

I've spent the last many years
writing good cheer
feeding people's fears
with hopes and dreams
touching the community
positively

well now it's time to up the score
as in 4 score and 7 years
when Lincoln dropped a proclamation
the emancipation of slaves
yet we live on grave times
gray skies stepping on land mines
to find our places to shine

Today, I speak of all people
to come together to create
a common bond
for some reason we don't all
grace the same stages
and today I ask for an upgrade
of human beings
to bring us all into the same phases

it starts before we leave our houses
with our children and spouses
the pictures of our own minds perceived
of how we view others positively
we teach our children through our own actions
they react to us creating their own reactions
once acted on, there are no retractions
just fractions of facts
based on assumption
presumed another person is bad
because of what generations have passed down

making rounds
creating hate crimes in our heads
instead of realizing God's plan
we should stand for the cause
but we choose to keep taking losses
holding human kind back
every chance the devil frets
he pulls off a win getting credit
for the drama

Today, I am on strike
laying my pen down on its side
until we all coincide together
fighting stormy weather
hand in hand
feet sharing the same sands
for aren't we all the same?

I don't give a damn about rainbows
for 40 days it has rained, more like
40 years times 40 million raindrops
killing the reproduction of future crops
to think differently on a clear day

some white people have to stop
thinking they are better
allow another person's ethnicity
to feel the wetter results of success
yeah, I see you shaking your head
we have come a long way and not everyone
thinks like you today
but we must all come to the conclusion
we live a delusion believing the bullisht
that all is okay

some black people have to lay aside
some hate and give in to fate before
it's too late
the world hates us because we hate
ourselves, as in all Americans

me born today can't be held accountable
for the things my people did

200 years ago
for so far we have come we roam
off course
divorced people cutting us all
in pieces
with a land to fill wondering who
holds the leases on life
finding us all under the blade
of a knife

as I said
I am on strike today
I lay my pen down
speechless with nothing to say
my ink has dried
my eyes have cried
with nothing more to say

The Paper Chase

the paper chase becomes a race of timing
where missing a moment will leave you
without shining
then you end up on the corner rhyming from
the heart on a soapbox trying to find some
money to feed your kids
living dime to dime got you blindly wandering
a grind where you seek to find a way out of
being down and out
you're even down on clout it makes ya wanna
shout to the heavens and ask God if you're
forgiven of the sins you committed because
lately when it comes to having your back, it
feels like He isn't with it

standing outside in the door waiting for some fiends to
hit the 1st floor where the score is made and you get
paid
you're just an Uncle Sam slave trying to make your way
and knowing you aren't the same got those you know
staying away
praying that God above will lead you to the light
cause they know you carry a gun if you had to fight
and they're praying on time just to make it right
because the paper chase is the only thing in sight

you're blind wearing blinders but you can't find her
the paper, the paper
people want isht for free due to the recession
pockets full of money, the economy just isn't
blessing and people running around stressing not knowing
when their next meal will be and in the midst of
it becomes crunch time and they need a fix
like a derelict, they commit something sick
to feed a habit just to get a hit
it's a robbery they enact adding to statistical
facts and the sad part
the government created the sickness

the government prints the paper that pays
for capers

and as problems taper out of control
the accounting becomes off balance and
the economics of supply and demand throws
the earth right off her axis
then to get control once again we have to go back
to basics and struggle to hustle as people
bustle and the state goes into debt paying
unemployment checks
poor people with degrees run around
breaking decrees that get them in trouble
as the crime rate doubles

America is greedy, it's all about the paper,
the paper
selling the car industry after years of wealth
crowned sitting on thrones
in Chinese American car horns are blown
thanking Americans for getting on their knees
to suck china d**k and a free pass to the throne
now we groan like we aren't grown as if we gave
away but instead we paved the way for the Communist
man to take it all away
now the money has blown in the air as we grab cab
fare to make our way back home

A Thug's Privilege

He put a shoddy to her body cause she was snotty
More snooty cause she wouldn't give the thug her booty
Looty, he did and stole her cream cause his mama
told him to never stop unless he buss a nut

Gotdamn, what?

yup *smdh*

You heard it like I did on the evening news where
many peruse the scene and rarely give a damn
It's a scam called life and the strife of trying to do good
young boys grow up too fast to fill the shoes of men when
they make a mistake that puts them in a place
as if they disappeared without a trace cause the green made them
greedy
That money doesn't buy you looks and a job
as a young girl abides by her family and looks the other
way instead of accepting his family

A young thug offers her dollars and logically the math doesn't
make sense and he robs her at least when
he should have left her alone for the best
The remains of her are the clothing on the street,
her panties marked with skeet and the shells that
suck her very last breath
He didn't just rape her, he took it to the death

The theft of innocence taking one's privileges
to walk so free in this society
Young kids have no chance to prance
through life to enjoy solo dances,
the little experiments that create a childhood
and raising up kids to be good
Before they hit double digits, it

becomes well known as statistics,
they are the very victims taken who die at
the hands of rage seen every day on the
front page of the Sometown, USA.

Love And Life

Lisa lives love and life,
loves life but her life doesn't
always have love

her father messed that up
asking her nervously one day
"what's up?"
looking at her funny
like he was broke
and she a pile of money
he said don't be shy
I just came by
to say what's up

the more he stood there
rocking to and fro
Lisa was seeking a way out
wondering where she could go
this man who helped conceive her
acted like she was captured
not going free

all of a sudden, he starts towards Lisa
and her mind counts to three

POW, BAM, BOOM

Lisa runs through the room
and up the stairs
he is chasing from behind and closing near
her biggest fear broke loose like a virus
she was worried for herself and her sisters
the heat of this left Lisa's heart blistered
wounded and broken
because this mother flower's actions were loud
and clearly spoken

Lisa's life had never been the same
because her own father hunted her
as his game leaving her ashamed
to have real love in her life...

Green Eyed Blues (inspired by NuEshe)

Let me tell you what I see through these green eyes
Can I tell you what I see through these green eyes?
I will tell you what these green eyes see
by race we differ, but can't help swearing
we live on the same streets
Homeless people and overfilled shelters
people begging for change running around
quite deranged out of their minds...confined
Chained to the drug that calls their name
no shame bowing to addiction
hooked like a snake under constriction
friction burning sensation from need
freed...indefinitely
to never succeed at life's dreams

My green eyes cry themselves dry
to see people wasting life indeed
never freed from the chains of their idea
of a civil liberty
civil, as in disobedience, to flee moral judgments
liberty, as in, free to do my own damn thing,
to lead a life of destruction defining a new day creed
Suicidal tendencies acted out so discreet
sneaking up on the weakness of society,
as a shadow to take the masses down in defeat

Can you feel the tears in my green eyes?
Let me tell you why there are tears in my green eyes
I will tell you what I see through my green eyes,
right now they are too blurred for you to see

Young girls believing the words of a young boy,
who swears he can love her as her man
to later pan out to a pregnancy for he got
between her thighs working his sweet talk
like calisthenics and exercise
by sex-ercising her mind blind to grind
S L O W—LYYYY to bleed
a seed between her legs
In the end, it's just her and what was produced
by his 3rd leg

Now she begs as he denies her cries committing
a crime of feeble mind who co-signed with a pen(is)
to conceive a child because of his wild style
He stands proud with a smile
a man (not)
To make money, he steals making an easy mil
to fill his piggy bank with easy bills always
chancing death or jail

My green eyes ache from crying as I tell you what
it is I see
I can't believe the lack of responsibility of people
with rights and liberties breathing to kill off the
masses so clearly we see

So Much (Pain) (inspired by Hollywood, Rick James)

Living in so much pain
with this wine in my glass
and things moving too fast
Looking at reflections of shame
sipping wine from the glass
wanting to kick my ass
How did this all come to be?
What was with all the fuss?
Did it lead to mistrust?
Was it really so much of
such and such?
Can't help but give it up
Don't know what to do
No desire to pursue it
no more

Sitting in the dark
with the glass in hand
I can't stand on my feet
because my knees went
numb
You used me like I was
dumb and respect went
out the window
as the rum coat my throat
your ego was bloated
a thing I noted in the back
of my mind
As attitudes grind the pain
to dust easily trust was the
ingredient missing

The mysteries of 2
histories relayed in stories,
where blistery pain's eye
can tell a 3rd story--the Truth!
2 angles from 2 sets of eyes as
1 laughs and the other cries
the 3rd eye draws the fine line
and learners of lessons fill in

the sidelines
cheering 2 fools on!

Living in so much pain
with this wine in my glass
and things moving too fast
Looking at reflections of shame
sipping wine from the glass
wanting to kick my ass
How did this all come to be?
What was with all the fuss?
Did it lead to mistrust?
Was it really so much of
such and such?
Can't help but give it up
Don't know what to do
no desire to pursue it
no more

Downing another gulp from
the glass
playing frames in my head
focused on moments so rash
trying real hard not to back
up and rehash
Just seeking facts to keep
perspective in tact
another sip, taste of lips,
bittersweet
One tear in the corner of
an eye, defeat
Love just wasn't enough
to fill in the hollowness of
the such and such that was
non-existent
Yes, that very much of something
needed I concede to agree you and I
just weren't to be
Living in so much pain
with this empty glass
I need to refrain from the
past just to continue breathing

Conspiracies Of A 3rd Eye

trilogy of my third eye
global fighter
with a pen as my weapon
scribing truths
sends the masses running
as though something stunning
came to be through me
like claiming to be the modern
day Jesus ¿que blasphemous?
so freaking ridiculous

as a creator
I breathed life into Jae Mo
a character with whom I flow
a gangster in the hood
representing as he should
drugs and killing
he makes the hood so thrilling
in no time he makes a quick million
without stealing

blucka, blucka, blucka,

another body drops
soils so spoiled and
can't grow crops
corrupted cops
allow crooks to buy into benefits
the screwed up system suggests it
keeping a shady man fit on the
street working his beat
to man the shadows and dark corners
feloniously
the shady corner strategies are endless
until the fall of one soldier
clouds my 3rd eye
leaving all mouthing the question
why?

it seems when someone fesses up
about how the cops messed up
dunking donuts becomes practice for the

drowning of a street warrior as tactic
knowing their dealings were raw
lacking a prophylactic
and a fireworks show becomes a
Star Wars movie gone galactic
leaving people dead
with one finger pointing at the feds
as the releasers of lead
when shells hit the ground
and bodies no longer stand around

the conspiracy

the feds want to know how Jae Mo came to be
through me
what seed was planted to help Jae succeed
at the underground game he runs so well
no shame
they need someone to blame and who with bigger fame
than Jae

he's as big as Diddy and Bad Boy
except the streets is his stage and a glock is his
toy
he got so big that he came off my page in 3D
and the police want to interrogate him so
intensely
they want to take him down and frame him
my phone is even tapped in case Jae calls me perhaps
the cops won't buy my milk and cookies bedtime story
of how Jae was created by my pen
scribed to drive hard and bodies in shards on the street
nothing discreet but when you look again
everything's cleaned up, no one speaks and all is
hush hush

the feds want Jae and claim all the crimes he's
committed will put him away
even as a character created, as a figment, of my own imagination
there's a fascination for the government
to want to see the acclimation of just another black man serving a
life sentence

Talking To Myself (inspired by Eminem)

Talking to myself
I hear a small voice of an elf
and answer as if cancer of the brain
ate at me
Seeing it rain pink elephants as I
rant about talking to myself and
attempting a vent to run the topic thin
Get sick of the utterance within
wanting clearance for takeoff because
stepping off the curb would do me in

Talking to myself as I sit back
because one voice
is intelligent and most considerate
engaging in some interesting isht
with a mentality quite fit like an athlete
Replay and repeat of the 1st round
and what should have gone down to have
all activity play out smooth, no sound
Damn, I am bought on some wine and pills
after I fought the will and that last voice
had skill so I gave in
When I drink, my thoughts are so clear
writing lines like "as alcohol numbs interference,
I mentally reference the relevant"
I gave consent for the voices that fill my head
to use those lines while under the influence
my pen went schizo and sold my talent
right out the side door of the family
They waited till I was too blind to see

I attempt to stand and head to the bathroom
where I further get consumed by conversation
looking in the mirror into bloodshot eyes I talk
to an old friend named Mind, who helps me interpret
some serious, heavy and devious meditations
Mind often gets caught up in the elation of laughter
He tells me I'm funny but Mind is the Master of
my thoughts
He gives me the best advice

I noticed after we spoke twice or three times
that Mind could advise as he guided but
he must be found at the bottom of a wine
or pill bottle
I give him the keys and he takes over the throttle
until I get myself straight
My words are louder than blood at a crime scene
I do bleed and my mind clots but when I cry
my thoughts bleed into words twisted
in rhyme schemes to hide incognito
not believing my absurd words could truly be
about me
I'm my own psychiatrist as inside my addictions
I enlist into an army where in darkness my struggles
bring me to a fork where when I can't decide,
I scribe as I drink and think until my Mind speaks
the Truth!!!

Slowdown Son (They Killed Him)

NYC skyline is the scenic background of my back yard that has
my back drop where
I go to poetically chop it up
Flowing with ole school rap and the sounds of beats that tap a
spine to want to grind
and stay on the game seeking the fame with the hottest lines
and ya hear Fat Joe saying slowdown son ya killin em as I speed
up my flow now
A 1 8 7 is radioed in an undercover ride as the murder team
creates a murda scheme to rile my dreams
All I need are the sounds of the city and the scent of something
gritty to get my pen ready to bleed these bars for the scarred who
survived and tell their story with a flow and some rhyme
It takes the neighborhood legend to lead them and put the hood
on the map
where people walk strapped because you never know what
wandering around a corner will getcha in the back
The boys in blue lacking men in uniform mentality running
rampant is the reality

slowdown son ya killin em, slowdown son ya killin em
as a 1 8 7 is radioed in an undercover ride

Dead on the corner
put him in the car and take him to the coroner in a body bag
A white flag goes up blowing in the breeze as a bullet flies by to
make some holes out of cheese
Slowdown son ya killin em

Ya got the mayors of the city
Jay-Z and Diddy giving out keys for free
It's about the almighty dollar and poppin ya colla
riding in a limo hanging out at parties just to be
seen
It's more than the lack of the towers to give the city power
It's a recession that keeps real people from spending real
money like it grows on a tree
The economy has to get better because all we see is rainy weather
in the spring
I need to hit up the dusty pawn shop to buy back my ring
Slowdown son, ya killin em

58

A woman at a red light gets a visit from an ugly face
It's a gun to her head and a get the heck up out the car
as she reaches for mace she's instructed to pull
down a dark alley in the light of day
She's dragged from the car, shot in the chest as she
signs the cross and they toss her in the trash
Slowdown son, ya killin em

Crash bang broom he's beat with a broomstick
because he's homeless they choose to pick with
a man who breathes to bother nobody
They choose to care and clean the sidewalk
from despair brought on by the nothingness
of this man
Yes, it's our boys in blue, we knew they
would show in this piece WTF? It wouldn't
be a poem without them showing up finally

Slowdown son ya killin him
as months later we enter the courthouse
where 3 louses who work for the city
walk free

Slowdown son, they killed him
and they still walk the beat

America, WTF?

The government is out to kill us all
on their own recognizance as they take
a stance but they don't see our fences
and the fight to go down
Our faces don't frown we smile so evilly
Terrorists aren't the only ones who can fold
some isht
Getting down in some grit got us, that make up
these United States, fit enough to get tough
with the best in it
Screw some rednecks and Tea Party bitches who got
the riches of the world in dollar signs to do their dirty
grind for the honor of a G Man's time
Who do you think pays for those extracurricular activities
as you bitches got your clits pierced
It's just a dog collar for a Bush rendezvous follower
that mother flower is still running isht from a place in
somewhere, Tx
As if his location would perplex us and not make us wonder
if Obama was the new stockade slave
the new face of American blame but that man has no
shame and I wouldn't place all blame because he has
no idea as he runs his agenda tame
He is the front man but on him Americans cannot
give the negative fame
it's the background fools dirtying the upfront jewels
Obama is the diamond in the rough that will drop it
tough for an economy zirconium bluff
he is the man to fix this problematic stuff that got
America cuffed by the sleeve
this Americans we must believe...

I Dreamed A Simple Dream (inspired by Poetic Devotion)

I dreamed a simple dream's dream
awaken to reality's horrific scenes
and on the edge of this dream I lean
out on the sill of reality
as I witness people screaming in the night
Isht isn't right
and taking in the outrageous site got me
pinching myself because we should all
be dead
Instead something frantic grips the streets
water fills every crevice with devastation
Unbelievable is the fall of this nation
the foundation of lies begins to crack
Plymouth Rock crumbles as the water
tumbles and levees can't hold back
the wall
A toll is being taken and for this right
now is what we are dying for
4 score and seven years, forget a politician's
career because right this moment, none of
us could care
Everyday and every step, do not be misled!
America, we are dying walking towards the death
The world is dying beneath our feet and the stench
of the rot is never sweet
Running the streets and not skipping a beat won't let
us reverse the issues at hand knowing the revolution
has waited too long to take that stand
The ozone been boned with the plague of aerosol cans
but we know it's more than that
The government backs it with scientific explanation
The globe has a fever suffering an infection of a back turned
impression
It's the responsibility of every country of this world to come
to a United Nation's peaceful arm's fold to talk about
keeping it green by helping 3rd World means
but it's a 'swept under the carpet' topic
Steering towards safety lacks the sense or know how
with Mother Nature on the prowl
and the rights as citizens of these United States
bears the weight of trying to stay afloat now

When you spend lifetimes helping others, who helps you?
If you're American in need, there's no big hand to squeeze
The world would rather see you drown suffering the
wrath of a Bush Rendezvous
than come through with a canoe to help you
I dreamed a simple dream's dream
awaken to reality's horrific scenes
and the schemes of just needing to breathe
cannot be conceived because someone will
even steal your free air
America, we are dying because we're on to
the next something or other like a cat with
9 lives, it's no surprise
I can't comprise my thoughts to believe the
greed of a world so big for so many people
that we now kill trees sucking away the oxygen
to now wheeze as if we all had asthma
Terrorism is quite a mental concept and when
we look in the mirror, there is bin Laden looking
back with the biggest attack on the ecosystem
ME, YOU, HE and SHE!
WE, killing off our very own environment in such haste
I dreamed a simple dream's dream and woke up to
that very scene...

Changes In The Game

Did you ever lose someone due to a price that was paid?
Turned around to be the one where the burden was laid?
Weight on your shoulders and the loss of a friend
makes you wonder if things would ever be the same again

The weight on your shoulders meaning the weight that the lost
one carried
He stayed committed to carrying it as though he and it were
married
now you miss him and no path to choose
at the moment it feels just like a game you would lose
What do you do and what do you think?
You try to make a connection by searching for that missing link

Enemies around you checking you out, wondering if your feelings
put you in doubt
to have confidence in the skills you possess
and carry the crew through to pass the next test
When he passed, the rules changed up,
and peeps looking like STFU.

He is gone and they think you are weak
and look at you like your future is bleak
It's like they think you are dead
and now you gotta come back with something
good instead

The next move is on you
and what will you do?
lay down and die
and let your ass fry
or get up, say STFU, and tell them why?

Kim Jong Who?

sitting on the throne
finger tapping patiently
next to the panic button
and the phone
waiting on the world
to swirl in his dreams

the masses scream for he now
has their attention
the crazy leader, Kim Jong II
flirts with Taepodong-2 missiles
for his own exhilaration
thinking he has the world
by the balls
he sits proud with the gall

what is he thinking and
what's up his sleeve?
not one thought can I conceive
but dreams of blowing up this
orb is the inspiration absorbed

question is, is he crazier than a
bin Laden fanatic?

he has caused some static
then he says, oh it's just testing
yet he's venting the fact
people may have forgotten the power
he holds so to prove a point
he scolds a cold world where people
turn to look but do they really care?
for he thinks he has dropped upon us
a dark scare

Worshipping Addiction

running up the block
with my hand on a glock,
looking for that man
who took off and ran
the one who beat me with a bat
because I wouldn't take all of that
isht he wanted me to believe
I asked him to leave
but he refused
acting like I needed to drop him a clue

after he beat me down and left me for dead,
he ran out the door instead
of getting paramedics to help me
it took my child to dial 9-1-1, see
he beat me down because he was lonely
suffering the addiction he has to the god of the crack pipe
it didn't make it right,
but he's sufferin'
needin' money,
cause he's lonely
yes, he's sufferin'

here I am a few weeks later
having healed
I'm walking the street looking for this man
the bills are due
the phone, cable and utilities were canned
what I thought he would do?
hell, now I needed a clue
with a husband like him,
I could do bad alone
but I felt I needed him because I was broke
and didn't have my phone

where was he?
suffering from his addiction of the crack pipe
stealin' and robbin',
just to get a hit
he didn't care it didn't seem fit
for a man with kids

and no food to eat
he was out runnin' the street
for a crack rock

further down, I saw sirens up the block
I started runnin' toward the scene,
hand still on glock
as I got closer, I heard the whisper of drug overdose
my heart racin' telling me it was my lose
glock hit the ground,
me runnin' around,
searchin' for information,
or the identification
of the body in question

could I get a peek?
he may be the one I seek

I was brought in the place where the body laid cold
I looked it up and down, he had grown old
yes, it was him
he was taken away before I could even get him,
yes, another victim of a crack rock

What Is To Come?

death is calling
it's in the air about
gray skies
people seek safety
wondering if this is a day
they will die
disease and death make up
much the stench
gators and snakes coming up
and attacking out of the trenches

looking to the heavens asking
does anyone care?
people are suffering on our homeland
and one thing I can't understand
we continue to fight in a far off place
that leaves us looking such a disgrace
in our own eyes

9/11 came and went and help was on the
way
because it was NYC, there was nothing to say
the money capital of the world was in dismay
Nawlins and Weasiville are suffering

human needs aren't being met yet we
have a damn president who lets the
problems become bigger and sends the
guards with guns locked and loaded ready to
pull the trigger
all this bullisht is just a smokescreen and to take
focus from helping people
deep down they want the real estate to build a
damn tourist attraction
so they drag their feet with aid

who the hell really runs this country?
I can't believe how priority is placed on
a life and idiots with power choose
to add on the strife
making taxpayers pay without shame

people need to rise up and help
the south is in a state of chaos and what
will come of the situations if they don't
get relief?

Still Not Getting It

Darkness enclaves a raven's realm
where an American flag blows in the breeze
shamed in the shadows of saddened mystique
The sharpness of black and white photographic
frames wheeze the stench of concrete gray
as they speak volumes to the masses that were gassed up
on black tie and suit affairs
The red, white, and blue and the 50 stars the stripes lay next
to should have fallen upon the stare of an albino man with
a color blind family and those not fooled
by the blindness already should have worn blinders
for head gear and grew sties in their eyes to recognize
the truth

9/11 came and went and people still aren't getting it
It lasted 2 weeks after the day the masked men stole
our security away
Stripped us of loved ones who faded away
above smoke and ash where their bodies decayed
and the survivors prayed hand in hand for better days
We must realize a rainbow is not just metaphoric
for the homosexual community
It's all of us who bring something to the
melting pot to brand it made in the U.S. of A.
We are not strays, who landed to be left stranded, on
a land branded by blood trails for the voodoo
spells to roam the land repeating history through
his and her story that may bore you because the
colors overwhelm and speak louder than your story

Getting lost in stories, a children's story and reading
to the kids as he got a look on his face gazing out
the window as words were whispered in his ear
The media tried to legitimize the crinkles
of concern round those eyes
but we all know despise was the true disguise
real people with clear eyes realize because
he knew he wined and dined with them
Terrorism struck holes in the humble abode
like swiss cheese
through airs of holey clouds that

stormed so gray
Now gray matter is the clatter that scatters people
who run for the black or white
Racism is the splat splat splatter
that shatters America's trust and
freedom to believe in religion and
ethnic pride to coincide since over
3000 people died
The resurrection of two towers at Ground
zero would be like 2 fingers in the air
The rise of a phoenix and America
the hero
but brothers and sisters, I can't take one
more step in the direction to resurrect
more bullshit
If we don't back up and direct attention
to the fact that because of this 9/11
situation
people have become suspicious of Arab
Americans,
as if they all danced with the devil in
the name of Allah and a holy Quran
re-written by some al Qaida mother
flowers who want all Americans dead

my response to threats from terrorists?
come get me Bitch!

Lord, if I'm wrong, please forgive me for
what I'm about to say
yes, I pray for peace in the place I stay
I also pray Americans would come to
an understanding that al Qaida isn't
trying to put a community center slash
Mosque so many feet from Ground Zero
I know and witnessed the crime committed on 9/11
I live across the bridge and saw the towers fall
I cried and my heart ached for days

When a soldier comes back from war cold in a box
the law says Fred Phelps and his freakin
Westboro Baptist church only needs

to be 150 feet to lurk
screaming shouts of fool and cruel insults
as a family grieves
A mother and father have to bury their child, that
isht is so wild but we give the terrorists a high 5
by depriving our rights as citizens to
worship as we choose, where we desire
It's like writing the 1st Amendment right
out of the Constitution
I guess the Bushs' had rights to dine with
the bin Ladens too
on 9/11, tower 1 on the 17th floor where
a Mosque resided, Americans died that
day!!!
THAT'S THE PART YOU'RE NOT GETTING!!!!

Militant Minds Freestyle (inspired by eNYgm@)

50 bullets and one life dies and no one pays a price and the victim was free to live a life of civil liberties
But on the day he was to take a wife she lay crying on his chest because hot lead took the best of him
Boys in blue and men in black stay close back to back with the detectives
Isnoras, Coopers, Olivers, the Justin Volpes, Kenneth Boss', Sean Carrolls,
Edward McMellons and the Richard Murphys of our times who also took
out the Philip Panels, Patrick Dorismonds, Johnny Gammages, Ousmane Zongos, Anthony Baezs, the Amadous and abused Rodney Kings and Louimas too

We have soldiers in another country fighting a war so we maintain
our rights but on our home turf our worth is isht because we have no idea why we are dying on city street's floors
Mr. Obama stays on stealth mode trying to figure out the problems of
the humble abode while creatures from the shadows and I speak of the wood of Mississip and Texas farmlands, where rednecks are having tea parties and having sex with their cousins giving birth to children that suffer being retarded

My word don't get me started because the produced being of such a union is not an excuse
but many run around in a recluse state free while the media screams the topic of terrorism on replay
Mentally deranged creatures hide in the wood on prey mode stalking a victim
because they're head is in a zone having received a subliminal message sent by God
that makes standing in sod fresh for the kill, as if a blessing was sealed at the altar of the sacrifice
The soldiers pay a price in foreign fields while the Timothy McVeighs and Terry Nichols plot in cornfields birthing the wet dreams of our government conspiracies that create mysteries pondered by the nightmares of past histories

Tell me please, what does it mean to be AMERICAN?

72

Is it a fight between 2 parties of democrats or Republicans?
My chin can't take one more tap after the thing 5 years ago in the
Bayou, where being American lost its 'show and prove'
as people died and those left behind suffered from the scars and
bruises on the mind that left many homeless needing to make a
new life and the tears from eyes that cried wouldn't help a tax
payer make it through a night from a day prayer lost its play
when a president gave those people a new name
and refugee was blurted without shame
AMERICA? WTF are we fighting for? I lost my train of thought...

We've Been Engraved With The 'X' (inspired by Poetic Devotion)

telepathy
surges an energy
poeticizin a fuse to my muse
that suffices the zeal of your zen
mend I do as you lend fortification
in the form of vitamin
time released so my pen will never
cease to beast the birth of a piece
deceased will be the weakness as it
decreases as Zeus breaks loose
to boost my alter ego

a poetic child with a wild style
where mile after mile, I'm fresh to
bang heads again and again and again

PD, you see, we be 1 of a kind kindred poetics
where schematics add up to more than mathematics
of rhythmic words squared
sister cancer unlike left foot dancers, we're advancers
in this word warrior world

2 pearls once rough like diamonds now wordsmith and war torn
from spit as we scream forget what Simon says
we stand on the edge of the world taking on phony
preachers, who swear they be teachers because of voices
they heard from a Being greater than you or I could conceive

yet we retrieve exact word message that came
as passages in dream form
from a God, the Father from whom we were born
"X" marked scalps, non-scarred and talcum smooth
as Father God proves He will use a poet to heal the
bruises of a cold, cold world
We've been engraved with the X

Children Of Liberty (inspired by eNYgm@)

Bin Laden is sitting in a cave while we been laden with
bodies in bags,
No resources and people being gagged with dollars
to keep mouths shut
instead of sticky duct tape to keep the quack from coming out
Americans have become stoked on stealth due to lack of
advancements on the healthcare issue
The best it gets is tissues to tears because despite our money
being good in the Capitol it becomes funny when used for
a common good

Look at our manufacturing industry, we became so broke we sold
the companies overseas while we still do all the work creating a
gross domestic product while someone like China does nothing
and earns a gross amount of dollars through the sweat and pain
of an American census

Then they turn around counting the reasons for lower crime and
the fact it will cost too much money if they encourage Americans
to give up smoking so they won't die
Living longer and rise in insurance claims are a fear that would
drain their pockets of OUR hard earned dollars

It doesn't take a scholar with a PhD to explain the administration
is blinding me and the latest smoke screen created was voting a
black man into the White House
Put him out front because he's a great speaker but they won't let
Obama preach because they don't want a preacher
He's black, was voted for president so what's the deal, like
his face on Wheaties, he's the mask of the presidential seal
Just be happy and shut the hell up

When another country suffers at the hands of Mother Nature
and we go off on words of a nursery rhyme singing "a tisket,
a tasket, a green and yellow basket" so we look so good
like we should on worldly level while we backstab our own
citizens who don't have jobs, suffer without food and
clothing
No consoling more like strolling nomadically through sands of
time along landmines waiting to blow up

and planes come home with body bags containing remains
reminding us we remain in a country fighting a damn war
looking for some guy named bin Laden that's been laden
on our shoulders while our own administration helps
him win a war

A Dear John Letter

you hunted me down
and thought my name
was hers
I even looked like her
and that left me scared
you taking the ultimate
I shook so delicate
after all was done
I had a fit no skit
lit you did a fire
under my feet
I ran
the sand couldn't cool
the skin of my soul

you messing with me
I had to break free
scary it was, keeping
it in the family
my eyes went blind, I
couldn't see until eye
realized the truth
you had no couth
the damage you did
there was nothing to soothe
talk about endings and nerves
like a knocked out tooth
the proof in the pudding
your print was the proof
it didn't take a sleuth
cause you could not have lied
to hell you will go and with the devil
you'll fry

as I sigh, eye close
my I to sleep
needing to count sheep
but the wolf eye peep
the fear seeps in deep
giving me the creeps
leap off a building

you bet I leapt
right to your death sentence
you got the penalty
where they pulled levers
my wordplay quite clever
was not the death of me
but of a dear john letter

Politically Untitled

Ameri-cain gave in to pain
as in Palin failin like a 6th
grader's shame
tossed in the towel, trowel in
hand digging the hole where
misery is polled, told are the
lies, not much surprise

the republicans don't have a leg
to stand after the entrance so grand
sand turned muddy, red carpet now
bloody
speak in detail, more as in code
morse by force, coerced isht
endorsed

what have I been saying?
a whole bunch of swaying isht
as republicans bob and weave
more than Ali in his day
avoiding the issues they got
tissues to eyes for they tell
so many lies avoiding the truth
for I have yet to hear proof
from their mouths to my ears
as to how they will do so many
things to calm our fears about
terrorism, homeland security,
the economy and how they plan
to dig us out of the recession we
now invest in, lessons learned are
never heard
swerve, curved like a back of scoliosis

boasted become the sideways glances
that leave camera eyes in trances as
John McCain stares at Sarah Palin
sexually harassing and stealing glimpses
of she as he claims it's all done in
victory
hugs and kisses, a sweet bit of bliss

he begins to cheat on the very woman
he cheated on his first wife with
ugly assed cold hearted man should be
shoved in that hole where I spoke of the
misery being polled
as for Mrs. Palin, she will need to deal
with all the necks where she stepped to
get where she's going
moving so fast, the ride can't last for if
elected
detected will be her fears if John McCain
dared to drop dead and leave her to run
the business

A Simple Revelation

The book of Revelations is but a dark cloud
that showers down from overhead
It was promised the earth would see bad
things in the final days
People's ways will put some teeth in that
ass and separating each and every class
The ones He was coming back for and
the rest that fell unworthy with hearts not
able to restore
Rich in money with pockets phat will not be
the richness He envisions
Wealth is what He's about in a spiritual form
and anything less will wash out with the storm
of the clean up
The faith of the mustard seed was all He asked
each one to have
Knowing we are hue man, He only requested
something we should've already had
Sad be the day when judgment falls
will it be the shower of the undying love or the
pits of hell where souls get buried alive at the
devil's door?
We choose our outcome in the way we live
knowing a being sent His only Son to give His
life for us has me looking at a mustard seed as
not too much to ask truly
We have to wake up and live right and as He
uses me as His vessel to get the message to
you think about the image of His visage on
your very last day and question if His face with
so many lines of stress got you wanting to
confess a great mess in that last moment
of breath

The Revolution Played Out

The breath of every person breathing is the push in the
movement for improvement
In life we are just students prudent to our plights
Though the revolution will not be televised, doesn't it get played
each day?
Right before our eyes, real life issues cannot be disguised behind
lies in the name of a movie title
Vital becomes life's lessons and a diligent learner avoids
digression in order to up the status of his/her position
Every day the revolution is televised before our very eyes
before the morning rises and way past sunset
We let seconds play out to minutes, minutes extend in hours
to years and the older this world gets, we have so much
reason to fret
From Osama bin Laden to Barak Obama, to the suicidal
bombings in Iraq, to the 911 attacks
Stacked are the problems going on in the world and
the death of families,
young boys and girls
Just in our country on U.S. sands, people are on our homeland
for the sake of freedom
Even Steven is but a figment of an imagination
Life is not fair when people wander nomadically, dying tragically,
magically some wake the next day thanking
God for another day to know the hurt and pain,
Blood stained truth that darkness cloaks their path—jobless,
homeless,
no food to eat to make it through another night, "oh, what a
treat?"
Defeat can't take you lower than belly gutter low
Slow be the government to care remembering some of these
people were taxpayers when thinking about the wrath of
hurricane Katrina
muddy bath waters wiping streets out like high tide, and
who can those people confide in when our president
had one word to describe their lives---
refugee was that word
They say the revolution will not be televised, what is all
this isht on the rise?
Seen on billboards, television, radio and on the street
The revolution is not discreet; it's loud and quite constant

One moment life is fine then it changes in an instant
it has no resistance and like a worn out rubber band, it SNAPS!!!
hopefully for the better

A Mother And Her Newborn (for Kamden and Shavon)

as mother holds her child
she can't hold back her smile
her love flows thick sooo smooth
this new born babe feels her style
the love only his mother could bring
as melodious as she sings to her new
born king
something stirs her heart as she craddles
and nestles him so close
she wants to be the most for her little man
promising him things right now he cannot
understand but when the time is right, he
will honestly comprehend her desires for him
and on a whim from the stirrings of his own
heart
mother and son will part once he grows into a
big man to take on the world
to raise his own little boy or girl swirled in candied
dreams
it seems a blueprint is a must and with the
Lord's help to trust the such and such's never
mentioned
but each footstep taken leads him on a venture that started
out with just a lil man and his mom holding tight

To the sweet dreams of a new day's dawn to a cold
dark world leaning each way for warmth
knowing God marked this child special to find
the path for his own spirit to blow around in the breeze
and his mother can grow old, no issues, pleased at
the success he breeds
and the blood that he bleeds to be royal like his Father
in heaven

L. K. S. (lifeknifestrife)

Life...Knife...Strife.....
she'd do anything to stop the madness
gladness never comes
young decisions leaves for later, a seasoned player
busted up incisions
scars never heal, just a reminder she was left
to deal
with answers she should never have asked the
questions of
she thought it was love but no white doves
fly overhead
instead it's dark clouds and ravens
no safe haven from issues
tissues all used and tears never dried
which she has cried for a long damn time
but being young she desired to feel wanted
and vowed in all seriousness she was ready
to commit to life, be a wife, the picket fence
but she lacked so much sense
no dollars or cents to afford things to buy for
the children she adored
floored broke, a stroke of bad luck, which without
gave the doubt of clout she was a loser at best
no zest, no good night's rest, she attested to confess
she made a true mess of her years
no time for a career
just pumping out babies till it was late, fate played no
hand for her name was Fate and she told on herself
shelved her body to be nothing more than a mere slave
to the rhythm she devoted her time to
raising those kids
and soon after she died, almost content

All In A Stare

I'm looking to be locked up
20 years to life
yesterday I was nothing more than a housewife
and today my back gets the knife

I lost control
and pressure took its toll
acting like I didn't know
and what I reaped was something I sow
now it was to jail I would go

the police put the cuffs on me
and at that moment my life did end
my quiet demeanor of surrender
gave no evidence of the message to be sent
all I knew, times up, my life is spent

sitting behind bars was a feeling so bizarre
far from that of a gazing star and a thought
I wanted to discard

the day you came to visit was more like a move
you used to outwit me
when they opened the door and we met eye to eye
the guilt on my face could not lie
in your heart the feelings for me died
I killed our child and could not deny
reality set in differentiating truth from lies

Cemetery Plot

one year later, Louisiana has become just a marker
of a cemetery plot
the spot where slots never opened up 6 feet under
I wonder sometimes as we live on dark times and lately
it takes more than landmines to wake us up
the president said it was taking longer to get money to
New Orleans, much more than Mississip
it's a trip how openly the government lies as though ties
to its own people don't mean a thing
they don't realize we see through that little lamb disguise
until our administration cries wolf
truth hurts when one blurts it out, loud and clear like the
cries heard from Tiananmen Square
Bush doesn't care but about dollar signs in his eyes and its
more than white light bringing the bling of a sun to shine
even Jay-Z has real estate on his mind for a 4040 club
the grub of a troubled town, word gets around but
the tower of Babel fell on Nawlins
buried not once but thrice round becomes compound for
interest
interest at best for undercover capers that taper down
to more than drips of more than tear drops to sobs
slobs are the G men who got choppy hiding behind a
suit and tie
they confide in an ear that leaks diarrhea of the mouth
about findings in the south
from rumors alone, how can one heal when active tumors
travel the walls of halls that became dilapidated from the
Lake Pontchartrain waters flooding hearts with darkness still
the pill is a placebo, the fake snake of a governments concern as
we learn in a place where freedom is birthright and tax payers
still must pay for a ray of sunshine of hope
to cope while the scope of the range of a firearm gets the
attention of killing civilians in a far off place that
disgraces a hypocrites heart
and scars are the veins to jumpstart a refugees will
on our own homeland still

a seed bleeds 2 succeed (for Ciara)

my seed bleeds 2 succeed assumption
proving that theory--
"making an ass out of you and me"
believe I do in the faces unveiled as
we drop bombs like hail
frail she may be but for all who can
see
she will leave you stuttering as her
limbs flutter and people mutter
in disbelief not even discreetly
making more of it public knowledge
that a child with less could get to college
the talk they speak leaves for a bloody trail
and a collage of negativity
talk is cheap and you can bleep yourself
without fail

call me sensitive I am but never lacking sense
to see and feel real
dumb asses will come correct and watch what
they say about people with challenges
some say disabled as though to dis the able
instead it's a dis on ability because
those with less amaze is the new craze
or fad becomes a child who puts a smile
on their mom or dad
my message to the few in the back pew
who boo
I thank God you didn't give birth to my
child for sense is just the beginning where
you are lacking

7 Days (about drug addiction)

Numb I am as the scum coats the walls as shit floats dirty water
like the Santa Maria of the seven seas as fleas infest a nest where
babes rest
I can't test my nerves any more as I am assed out floored as if my
cries go ignored to plead the words you read on my lips as you
take acid trips that skip days, months and
years and awakening to tears is the best it gets
I fret as if I let all you live inhibit the internal workings of your
mind as if you were
fried egg blinded by the blinders that fog uses to clog arteries of
pulses deadened as
if heaven's beat reached out so far to be your lifeline's fray as you
can be blessed to wake another day
Wasted and quite erased becomes yesterday as the second day
enlightens frightening facts of consumption through assumption
that abuse can loosed her noose to allow you
to breathe relieved of suffering
The mothering of years gone bad are saddened scenes that take
ten steps back as attacked is the being as seething pain rears its
head
Instead the clues were brighter than Blue's and louder than a
loud crowd's boos
you were too deranged to catch the message arranged along your
path
where doing math had you bypassing class
Escaping the tape of back door's seal where food for thought gave
you a meal
but starving became your grieving demeanor and leaner thoughts
get caught up light weight
As if to skid over ice u not weighed to persuade you to think
a different way on the third day
The fourth day becomes a word day where wrought iron meaning
is scheming to scold a bold topic to stop it from tearing us apart
But from start, a loving heart with a firm hard love theme is the
meaning of my content which sent chills up my spine
in supine rhyming
Dying to climb the shoulders of mimes to silently send prayers to
the skies
where ears of gods are rattled with riddled insanity and
day 5 comes after the fight of a long hard night is quieted by
daylight's knock to block a darkened core

Day 5 is like rebirth being reborn after being scorned in a world
so torn as society's back gets attacked by the chimp intact
Not letting go and messing up the flow of preaching that is spit
outreaching to screech the brakes to a halt
The 6th day defines your sin within
you are full of chagrin but on the outside so far is your
denial as you run 100 miles fast not letting up on you running
out of gas
Oppression overshadows shallow promises as doubting Thomas
redefines your spine as weak and you fall broken
No words spoken but the actions taken could set you up
for the seventh day
I call upon the help of God to pull you up and out of dirt and
weeds to soak you in the sod of blessings
where guessing does not play so crude and rude games where
lameness is just a way
But backing up to replay the scene we've seen where all involved
has suffered you see and health is restored like the
day before day one

One Second Changes Everything

Walking down the block, I see a gig about to rock,
in the neighborhood where I stood, like a fire alarm
I had no idea what I should do since stuck in the middle holding
the hand of you know who
Yes, the dude I had been seeing when the shots rang out
People were running all about and all you hear are screams
and shouts
Everyone scrambles taking gambles without a doubt
For me, all of a sudden my body froze and
my hearing was gone, as I lay upon the ground
blood squirting out of the wound, unable to move
My body feeling bound like I had been tied
not moving, just there on the ground where I lied
My eyes took on a glazed stare even though I
could see my body getting cold and something wet
ran down my side
how could this be?
Did the Lord want me now?
Have I finished all His work that was assigned to me?
I laid there staring blank while everyone above me was
running around as though they didn't see me on the ground
For all it was worth, I could see my spirit had already left
this earth
I was not scared but well aware that my time was up
and would be going home to be left in the Lord's care

Some BS Racism Spiel

tharealone, the steel onepens words that bite
the words read tight
then take flight
on the wings of an angel
to the masses
so you can see, it's a revolution
so put on your glasses
because my message trashes
any rumor that passes
through your ears as
they steer in the wind

my scribe is gospel
backed by counsel
this color isht has to stop
it's a new day
with better things to top

the crap going on in the world
needs to be tied to a rock
and tossed in the ocean
the witches brew of a new
potion is desired
racism needs to hang up a
number
cause its retired
after setting everything a fire

further down the road
the people need to live
different
and act like they know
we need a euphoria
of an afterglow flow
that of a halo
to prove we're better than that isht
we have lived since the beginning of time
an angelic aura of something more
we can adore to up the score
and raise up the human race

I pen rhymes to spark a mind
open your ideas that
were confined
and let them air out
in due time another brain
will shout as the revolution
gets fueled like a train
food for thought
in a message we get caught
up in feeling
then we can begin dealing
refreshed like an after dinner
mint with healing

Abortion: A Chilling Thought

killing is abortion
the money's extortion
just to keep a secret quiet

outside the clinic
people plan a riot
girls walking in
are still down with it

the guy involved doesn't even know
because she walks in alone
he doesn't even show

the baby never had a chance
even since conceived

she walked in herself
and left relieved
for the baby is destroyed
as result of the act

her parents never know
what their baby's been through
between you and me
it's just a point of view

Broken Mold Of A Ghetto Bastard

born a ghetto bastard, young Troy already defeated before his
chance to master, Life Skills 101
his mother being his teacher, the one he would learn from
she was no better because of the place of that she came meaning
Troy is just a repeat of generations to go down in defeat
living years of deceit had them hoping for better down the road
instead they lived a sad life that taught one to grown old
his mother had some cracks, which labeled her a broken mold
and never was good enough for her own seed to break free
free of the chains of the creed that left them mentally confined as
defined by society that held them down
already diagnosed, as brain dead has left them buried in the
mind, six feet underground.
his father abandoned his mother and never stayed around to
make a bit of difference to raise his son to be a man
instead Troy learned how to hate his father on instinct at the
sound of his name
leaving a woman to raise his seed should have brought him
shame
knowing exactly how it looked to be called lame
he never learned a lesson to avoid producing more offspring and
failed this very game
Keith was born a ghetto bastard behind his brother, Troy, having
been left to master Life Skills 101...

Haunted By The Game

Jae Mo lay in the bed sweating, not able to breathe
he sat up, shirt drenched looking for relief
grabbed the cross on his chest asking
God, what's going on?

eyes still blurred when the vision appeared but by the time
he could see it was gone
wondering what it was before his eyes
he dug under the pillow for the glock 40 and couldn't find
it to his surprise

by the time, he was fully awake,
Jae wondered if what had passed was real or fake
could his mind and eyes make such a mistake
to believe what they had seen?

ah, never mind and being so alert,
he decided to take a shower and go for a ride

out on the street driving his black Benz,
his vision was more focused and his body less stressed
more relaxed in the clothes in which he was dressed,
he was staring at his image in the rear view mirror in
between peeks at the road
his own impression was that of the very fact he had
grown old

one more look in the mirror sent the car into a swerve,
trying to control the wheel to make it through the curve
Jae Mo pulled over to the side of the road to his disbelief
he shot around with the glock in his hand saying it could
not be a repeat of the image he saw of the woman that he
killed right out on the street

she died a crack head's death because she could not pay
he aimed right between the eyes as her children watched
mesmerized
the dealer pulled the trigger and did not care to
realize all the changes he would make in the
children's lives the kids watched,
gun was shot and mom's body dropped

96

Jae Mo thought that was it
from the grave, she came back to get him because
he left her children to cry without a mother by
their side

he could fool himself for a little while
saying the event did not bother him but that was a lie
when it came to those kids, he heard their pleas and
how they cried

he looked the mother in the eye
as she spoke her last words to him
she uttered, "From my grave, I will make you pay
and get the chance to watch you die"
that haunted image left him so scared and he knew
damn well this woman would make him fry...

Dirty Mind

he could be seen roaming the streets everywhere
and when he came upon me, we would stop and stare
even though I was 15, he stood there and often grabbed
at his crotch and in amazement I should stand there
and watch
I knew exactly what he wanted because he never fronted
he didn't shock me nor was my growth ever stunted
he amazed me, as my feelings overwhelmed
the emotions, they were shunted
through my veins leaving guilt as the stains
along the walls of these veins
of my desires and feelings
it wasn't about him but about IT
referring to the dealings
that would hurt and conquer my heart
breaking me all apart
this thing I call IT was the rape
it's a nightmare that fills my head and I cannot escape
because he text messaged me on my two way
trying to get me to come with him to play
a sick man's game
that once he was caught will leave him looking
lame bringing negative fame to his name
but back to this distant picture at hand
and looking at this man as though I understand
what it was he wanted from me
and listening to him calling me even though running
would set me free
when my two way went off I picked up
and it was his voice that came off of the text that
I read saying what's up?
asking do I have time for him today
he really looked forward to play
having me in his very own way
well, things got a bit rough
it led to a struggle making it very tough
to get away from him forcing me to put up a fight
but to fuck me was what would be his delight
making life in his eyes alright
that was the last day I had been seen
leaving the rest of the story a bad dream

the only thing found to prove of my whereabouts
was the two way that was found out
in the garbage near the street
where I put up a fight and tried to plea
with no possibilities to flee
and now I am gone and you know the end
of the story

Without A Care

The fire chief was going over his report in detail
with the detective, who was out seeking the suspect who
would go to jail
They knew who he was even though the mother was no better
The father of the kids was out to get her
The mother who left the kids unattended,
had to work and no one to watch her poor children
She left them alone while she went to work
It seemed their father got tired of paying support
and to be a jerk set the house on fire
Making the mother look like a liar
but he didn't realize that a neighbor saw him start
the fire
pouring gasoline like a hit man for hire,
She knew it was him by the way he limped
He was known through the hood as a playa pimp
A real lady's man but was he really a man?
He knowingly killed his own flesh and blood
to save paying out a few bucks in order to raise the kids
Now his actions will put him on death row
while the kids lie dead with no chance to grow
The mother will also spend time in jail
and she will never really know what this man
possessed to pull off what he did
to keep from spending money on his kids
The fire chief told the police detective it was
such a shame that children had to be victims of
his ruthless game

Just Another Day

A young boy enters a corner supermarket to rob and
he comes out in a body bag, never mind the fact that
he didn't have a job
Society would never hire him because he has a record
longer than his arm because he was running loose
robbing and thuggin doing people harm
His name was Drew now that you heard his story,
you want to act like you knew?
Too bad it's too late
His body is headed six feet under and frozen cold,
dead to the world before birth as a fetus in the womb
The day he was born was as dark as Halloween filling
his first day with gloom
He had no positive role model in his life to teach him
right from wrong
His young twelve years should have been happy instead
of full with negativity making life so long
Due to mental obstacles and a weak mind his backbone
was not strong
No one reached out with a hand to save this young man
He died knowing hatred, selfishness, and being poor
Drew never got a second chance in order to restore
his life to some decency
He was out of control since infancy having been
born to a life with no mother and nine brothers
His mother existed in between hits on the pipe and
selling her body to feed the habit
Other than that she was a diamond in the rough not
knowing the size of the carat
with nine brothers and ten fathers, there was no
man in the house because they were men who could
tell you how to get into a woman's blouse
Never mind raising a family and being the
head of the house
Then you come back to the scene in front of us
where a young boy gets blown away and life goes on
like another day

People...why?

the fist of black power is outdated.
racism seeks new heights agitated
the government is organized crime
controlling races making minorities do time
the fine line has evaporated into thin air
while the majority cheers
when are we as a whole going to drop the bullshit
and bring on 2004
people are allowed to knock on your door
asking if some type of god has been there before
our society worries more about the way it looks
the millions of memberships at gyms across America
is the truth
it's so bad, Catholics sit in church on Sunday doing
calisthenics in the pews is the proof
Latter Day Saints walk blocks everyday trying to push their
beliefs
Jehovah Witnesses tapping on window glass to get membership
into your heart trying to tell you your God is a lie
I get mad and push the table on its side about to tell them why.
Why? Why? Why?

Why can't people just be people and their soul be considered the
temple where God resides?
Why can't my color not represent past lies based on history but
represent me, the one living in this lifetime?
Why must we, as whites and blacks, be separated by the fine
line?
Why must we be held accountable for what other whites did that
created bad ties?

shoot, I am one person minding my own business doing my part
to help the healing start.
Why do I have to be hung on a tree because of past animosity
that the topic of racism brings?
damn, today we all should be the kings and the queens
in this society.
religion is the root of evil instead of the stirrings of some
productive re-growth
shoot, people feel dissed when how they look leaves them

looking stupid instead of kissed by cupid.
if you are out of shape, fashion doesn't live in your house no more...
you need to lose weight to up the score.
life isn't fair and there are more fair-weather friends instead of ones who care.
Why can't what I just spit be something left as a mark on your mind instead of a spark to start some isht added to the rest of time?
When will people be people accepted as people and your heart be a church steeple and the way you look be held in the eye of the beholder?

Tammy Jones~~Poetry's Child

Contact Information:

Email:
tammyjonespoetry@yahoo.com

Phone:
(973) 494-6014

Other works by Tammy Jones

"Floetry Of The 3rd Eye"

It can be found on the Publish America site:

http://www.publishamerica.net/product3895.html

***Look forward to the release of Tammy's third book, "Something's In The Air" with updated information coming soon.